JAGUARS

by Arnold Ringstad

amicus
high interest

Amicus High Interest is published by Amicus
P.O. Box 1329, Mankato, MN 56002
www.amicuspublishing.us

Library of Congress Cataloging-in-Publication Data
Ringstad, Arnold, author.
  Jaguars / by Arnold Ringstad.
     pages cm. -- (Wild cats)
  Summary: "Presents information about jaguars, their habitats, and their special features, including their swimming skills"-- Provided by publisher.
  Audience: 6.
  Audience: K to grade 3.
  Includes index.
  ISBN 978-1-60753-601-7 (hardcover) -- ISBN 978-1-60753-641-3 (pdf ebook)
  1. Jaguar--Juvenile literature. I. Title.
  QL737.C23R567 2014
  599.75'5--dc23

                                2013049436

Photo Credits: Pal Teravagimov/Shutterstock Images, cover; ostill/Shutterstock Images, 2, 12-13; Matt Gibson/iStockphoto/Thinkstock, 4-5, 23; Dr. Morley Read/Shutterstock Images, 6-7; biosphoto/SuperStock, 8-9; SA Team/ Foto Natura/Minden Pictures/Corbis, 10-11; Krzysztof Wiktor/Shutterstock Images, 14-15, 22; Tom Brakefield/Corbis, 16-17; Joe McDonald/Corbis, 18-19; Matt Gibson/Shutterstock Images, 20-21

Produced for Amicus by The Peterson Publishing Company
and Red Line Editorial.

Designer Becky Daum
Printed in the United States of America
Mankato, MN
January 2015
PA10006
10 9 8 7 6 5 4 3 2

TABLE OF CONTENTS

Fur and Spots

Jaguars are the biggest South American wild cats. Most have tan or orange fur. They have black spots. Spots help them hide in forests. Some jaguars are all black. They are called **panthers**.

Fun Fact
About six out of 100 jaguars are black.

In the Rain Forest

Jaguars live in **rain forests**. The cats stay near rivers. Some use caves as **dens**. Others make dens under trees.

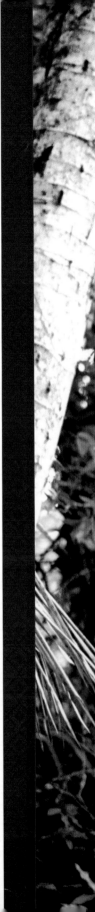

Big Cats

Jaguars can weigh up to 260 pounds (118 kilograms). They have big paws. This helps them swim. They also have sharp claws. This helps them climb trees.

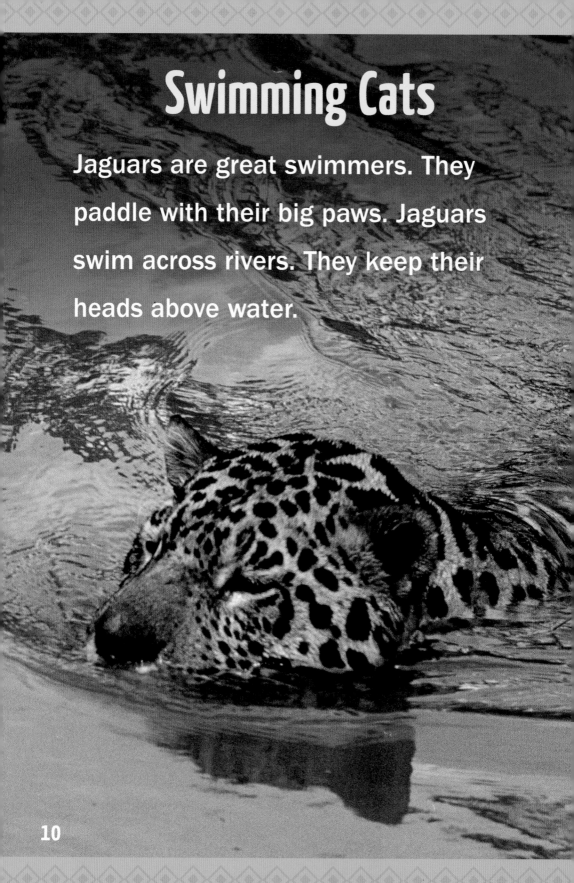

Swimming Cats

Jaguars are great swimmers. They paddle with their big paws. Jaguars swim across rivers. They keep their heads above water.

Like a Housecat?

Most housecats do not like going in water.

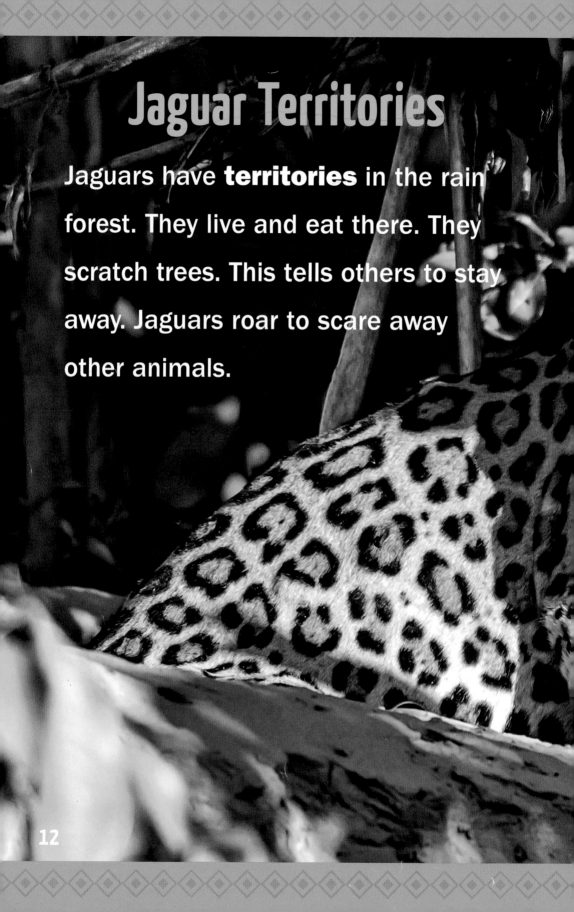

Jaguar Territories

Jaguars have **territories** in the rain forest. They live and eat there. They scratch trees. This tells others to stay away. Jaguars roar to scare away other animals.

Like a Housecat?

Sometimes housecats scratch furniture.
This is similar to how jaguars scratch trees.

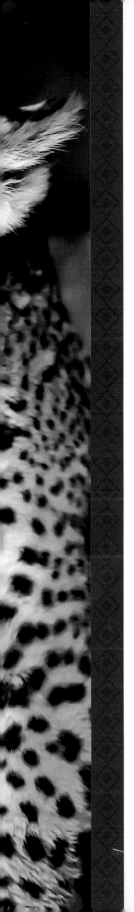

Little Jaguars

Jaguar cubs weigh less than 2 pounds (0.9 kilograms). Their mother protects them. The cubs grow fast. After one month they weigh 7 pounds (3.1 kilograms)!

Learning to Hunt

Jaguar cubs live with their mother for two years. They drink milk for six months. The milk comes from her body. Later, she brings them meat to eat. She teaches them how to hunt.

Hunting in the Forest

Jaguars hunt fish and turtles. Sharp teeth let them bite through turtle shells. On land they hunt **capybaras**. Good eyesight helps them see prey at night.

Fun Fact

Jaguars wave their tails over water to fish.
The fish swim to the surface.

Far from People

Jaguars live in Mexico and South America. Most live in the Amazon rain forest. The cats live far from people.

Jaguar Facts

Size: 150–300 pounds (68–136 kg), 60–72 inches (150–185 cm)

Range: Mexico and South America

Habitat: rain forest

Number of babies: 1–4

Food: fish, turtles, capybaras

Special feature: large paws for swimming

Words to Know

capybaras – South American animals that look like large guinea pigs

dens – places animals use for shelter

panthers – a jaguar, leopard, or cougar with black fur

rain forests – warm, rainy areas with many trees

territories – areas animals live in and defend

Learn More

Books

Ganeri, Anita. *Jaguar (Day in the Life: Rain Forest Animals)*. New York: Heinemann, 2010.

Guidone, Julie. *Jaguars (Animals that Live in the Rain Forest)*. New York: Weekly Reader Early Learning, 2009.

Websites

National Geographic—Jaguars

http://animals.nationalgeographic.com/animals/mammals/jaguar

See photos of jaguars and hear the sounds they make.

San Diego Zoo—Jaguars

http://animals.sandiegozoo.org/animals/jaguar

Read more fun facts about jaguars.

Index